SUPERBASE 16
KANEOHE BAY

SUPERBASE 16
KANEOHE BAY
The Marines' Hawaiian Haven
Steve Mansfield

This book would not have been possible without the full co-operation of the US Marine Corps, and I would like to thank everyone at Kaneohe Bay and Marine Corps Headquarters whose assistance made my job so much easier. A special mention must go to Major Kerry Gershaneck and the staff of the JPAO at K-Bay for their hard work, particularly SSgt Christopher Grey who was an adaptable, friendly and efficient link to the various units on the base. And I would also like to acknowledge the help given to me by the Station Operations and Maintenance Squadron, especially Capt Roy Kompier, and the crew of the Flight Clearance office.

I must also thank Nikon UK Ltd, and John Pitchforth in particular, for help with equipment. All the photographs in this book were shot with Nikon cameras and lenses.

In common with many military installations, MCAS Kaneohe Bay is a closed base. To enter the base you must have a valid reason for being there and the visit must be arranged in advance.

Published in 1990 by Osprey Publishing Limited
59 Grosvenor Street, London W1X 9DA

© Steve Mansfield 1990

British Library Cataloguing in Publication Data
Mansfield, Steve
  Kaneohe Bay.
  1. United States. Marine Corps. Military aircraft
  I. Title   II. Series
623.74′6′0973

ISBN 0–85045–970–2

Editor Tony Holmes
Page design by Richard Winnington
Printed in Hong Kong

Front cover A dissected 'Frog' on the Kaneohe ramp. The abundance of hatched maintenance panels on the venerable CH-46 aid the groundcrew immensely when servicing this weary workhorse between sorties. This camouflaged CH-46E belongs to HMM-262

Back cover While the 'groundie' gives the nose gear the final once over, the pilot completes his preflight checks. This particular F/A-18C is the personal mount of VMFA-232's commanding officer, hence the colourful 'Red Devils' motif just forward of the cockpit

Title pages Visiting RF-4s taxi on to the runway to start the second leg of their journey home to El Toro, California. Kaneohe Bay is an important stopping-off point for Marine Corps aircraft crossing the Pacific

Right A CH-46E crew prepares to take-off. The venerable Sea Knight, the Marine Corps' ubiquitous cargo helicopter, is the most common type of bird on the Kaneohe Bay ramp

For a catalogue of all books published by Osprey Aerospace please write to:

The Marketing Manager, Consumer Catalogue Department Osprey Publishing Ltd, 59 Grosvenor Street, London, W1X 9DA

Introduction

On 7 December 1941, Japanese forces struck a blow against the United States which propelled both countries into World War 2. The first bombs fell not on Pearl Harbor, however, but on a small Naval Air Station just over the mountains, in Kaneohe Bay. The aim was to knock out the station's aircraft—mainly PBY Catalinas—before the main attack began on the fleet at Pearl, just minutes later.

The beautiful Mokapu Peninsula, on the southeast side of Oahu, Hawaii, first became home to naval aviators when a small seaplane base was built in 1939. But its history goes back much further. According to Hawaiian legend, life on Earth started when the gods created Man from the sands of one of its beaches. There are ancient burial grounds here, and the Nuupia Ponds, which virtually cut off the peninsula from the rest of the island, are ancient fish farms.

The isolation appealed to the Marine Corps which started occupying the area in 1953 with a Marine-Air Ground Task Force. By 1956, airfield operations at Marine Corps Air Station Kaneohe Bay were in full swing and the task force became the 1st Marine Expeditionary Brigade, a vital part of the Fleet Marine Force, Pacific (FMFPac).

The remoteness is good news for non-military occupants, too. The security of the base provides protection for many species of wildlife. The Marines' care for the land they inhabit has resulted in the Air Station picking up eight conservation and environmental awards. And they also win the gratitude of local and visiting bird watchers who have enjoyed the base's frequent wildlife tours.

However, the main activity on the Peninsula is strictly military. The 1st Marine Expeditionary Brigade is a unique outfit within the Marine Corps in that it has all types of unit, from grunts to zoomies, all gathered in one place. Headquarters units, fighter squadrons, helo squadrons, infantry, amphibious assault units, artillery and recon units all train and operate together.

Aviation is the province of Marine Air Group 24. Fast jet operations are taken care of by three fighter/attack squadrons—VMFA-212, -232 and -235—who early in 1989 traded in their old F-4 Phantom IIs for brand new F/A-18C Hornets. Helicopters are even more numerous, with one CH-53D Sea Stallion squadron (HMH-463) and four CH-46E Sea Knight squadrons, HMM-165, -262, -265 and -364.

The 1st MEB's main ground combat element is the 3rd Marine Regiment (Reinforced), the largest infantry regiment in the Corps. They're backed up by Brigade Services Support Group 1 (supply, maintenance, transport and medical battalions) and the 1st Radio Battalion.

One of the Brigade's major roles is in support of the Marine Prepositioning Ships programme, where container ships loaded with equipment and ordnance patrol strategically important parts of the world. If trouble flares up somewhere, the Corps simply rendezvous with the ships, picks up its gear and goes into action.

The other main tenant on the base is the Naval Ocean System Center, a research, development, test and evaluation laboratory. MCAS Kaneohe Bay is now home to 15,000 Marines, sailors and their families, who enjoy this idyllic environment of sun, sand, surf and fast jets.

Contents

Right A VMFA-212 Hornet taxies back to the hangar after a training sortie

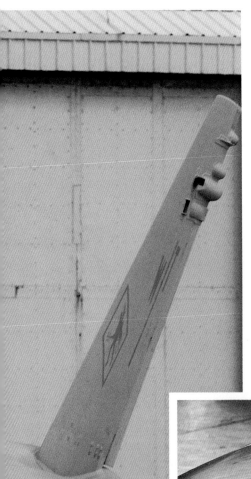

Hawaiian Hornets

Left The F/A-18 Hornet is a versatile machine. It's replacing both the F-4 Phantom II and the A-7 Corsair as a dual role fighter/attack aircraft. That has led to criticisms of it as a 'jack of all trades, master of none'. And its operational radius of around 740 km is said by some to be too short for a carrier-based attack plane. Yet the Hornet quickly wins friends among pilots for its agility and handling. The prototype, the Northrop YF-17 Cobra, was a competitor for the USAF Air Combat Fighter programme, but lost out to the F-16. The Navy liked the look of the aircraft, and appointed McDonnell Douglas as the main contractor to develop it as the F/A-18. The machines at Kaneohe Bay are all C-models

Below The large leading edge extensions (LEX) running from the wing under the cockpit, give the Hornet a hybrid wing, providing increased stability at high angles of attack and better handling at transonic speeds. They also act as compression wedges, reducing air speed into the engine intakes

Inset The exhaust nozzles of the General Electric F404 engines are fairly small, making the aircraft less conspicuous and helping to keep down its infrared signature

Left Reliability is turning out to be one of the Hornet's strong points, apart from early problems with the engines. Maintenance personnel who used to coax extra life out of the F-4s have comparatively little to do, and many have been reassigned to other jobs. This newly-arrived aircraft is waiting to get checked out before joining its companions in VMFA-232

Above Maintaining the Hornet could hardly be easier. Want to know where the problem is? Just ask the computer. The Built-In Test Equipment system provides information about faults on the cockpit multi-mode display. Most of the avionics are built around line replaceable units, which can be quickly swapped. Getting inside is easy, too, as the aircraft has 307 access doors, over half with quick release latches, and most accessible from deck level

A Hornet waits in the rain for its turn to refuel in the high-speed pits. K-Bay has
four refuelling pits, although it generally uses only two at a time, as most
missions are two-ship sorties

The high-speed pits are capable of pumping around 2000 gallons of JP-5 into a thirsty Hornet in just five minutes. Turnaround time can be even less if they are just filling their internal tanks, which have a capacity of 1620 gallons. And it's not just Hornets—most other types of aircraft are customers for the pits

Left Aircraft on training sorties often carry out a hot turnaround, where they fly one hop, return, refuel and launch again without ever turning off the engines. In-flight refuelling isn't normally available to K-Bay's aircraft, so the pits are heavily used

Above Refuelling doesn't stop for anything. Downpours are common in Hawaii, but generally short-lived. The salt-laden atmosphere is more of a problem, and creates most of the maintenance headaches

Above left One of VMFA-232's aircraft gets a once-over from the ground crew before a hop. At the time the pictures were taken, the 'Red Devils' had only half their complement of aircraft, and their sister squadron, VMFA-235 'Death Angels', had yet to receive their first!

Below left Col Gary Elsten, MAG-24's commanding officer, climbs aboard his aircraft. As a single seater, the Hornet puts a greater work load on the pilot than two-seaters like the Phantom II. But this is largely alleviated by the fly-by-wire controls and the glass cockpit, which prevent the pilot being overwhelmed

Right Col Elsten's wingman for this sortie is Lt Col George Tullos, VMFA-232's commanding officer, who is waiting for the signal to go before closing the canopy and taxiing out to the holding point. The two-piece canopy gives excellent visibility, and is designed so that the front part hinges upwards, giving access to the instruments for maintenance

Left Strapped into the Martin-Baker Mk 10L 'zero zero' ejection seat, Col Elsten starts his preflight checks, aided by the on board computers

Part of the Hornet's agility is due to its small size and weight. The fuselage is mainly aluminium, but graphite/epoxy materials are used extensively, especially on the tail, elevators and wings. This is largely a result of McDonnell Douglas' experience with the Harrier II

A VMFA-212 Hornet rolls back to the ramp after a sortie. It was probably a long mission as the aircraft is carrying a 315 gallon drop tank on the centreline hardpoint

Above A pair of Hornets start their take-off run, as seen from the control tower. Although it's a small runway, tandem take-offs are the norm

Right A Hornet driver lights up the burners of the twin F404-GE-400 engines as he launches on a night hop. This low-bypass turbofan was developed specially for the Northrop P-530 (YF-17) Cobra, the direct predecessor of the Hornet

Inset One of the main improvements made when the YF-17 developed into the F/A-18 was the general beefing up of the undercarriage. The original was fine for Air Force-type operations out of airfields but hopeless for the rigours of carrier life

The Hornets' wingtips invariably create vapour trails, thanks to Hawaii's humid atmosphere

Above Lancers 00 and 11 launch prior to performing 'pig in barrel' intercepts. When these pictures were taken, VMFA-212 was running about six sorties a day, each with two or four aircraft, while the crews built up their experience with the aircraft

Inset A Hornet driver from VMFA-212 gets his wheels up as he roars out on a training sortie. Typical training missions include ordnance and fighter weapons, photo reconnaissance, and suppression of enemy air defences

Main picture Still using full afterburner to get his speed up, a 'Lancer' blasts out. Reheat is also used to boost the Hornet's speed to its maximum Mach 1.8

Above Neatly summarizing the changes that had just been wrought at K-Bay, a Phantom II (actually an RF-4C from VMFP-3 based at El Toro) prepares to leave while a Hornet arrives. Beyond the end of the runway are the waters of the bay, and beyond that mountains. Arriving aircraft approach the strip in a descending turn

Right Without stores on the hard points, the Hornet leaps off the runway in just a fraction of the space taken by the earlier Phantoms. The noise level is considerably lower, too

Above The Hornet's role as a carrier-based aircraft is revealed by the folding wingtips, used to conserve space. However, the Hornet is already a compact aircraft

Right Halfway along the nose, just above the radar bay, is the gun port. The fuselage provides a home for the M61A1 Vulcan 20 mm cannon and a 570-round ammunition drum

A VMFA-232 'Red Devils' bird sucks power from a mobile generator whilst the ground crew performs pre-flight checks. However, the Hornet does carry an auxiliary power generator, which is used to provide juice for the computer and avionics systems during maintenance

The unusual twin, angled tail fins help reduce the Hornet's radar signature and eliminate effects of body vortices at high angles of attack. Early production versions of the Hornet suffered stress problems on the tail fins, but the problem was solved with small strengthening plates

Above left The once gloriously heraldic markings of fast jets have now been reduced to the monotony of air superiority grey with low-visibility markings, as shown by the tail of this VMFA-232 'Red Devils' Hornet. The yellow-green stripes are formation lights

Above right The bumps at the top of the tail of this VMFA-212 aircraft are: a navigation light, antennae (including a rear-facing radar warning antenna) and, just above the rudder, the square fuel jettison pipe. The small, square reinforcing lugs are also visible near the bottom of the fin

Right K-Bay's Hornets sit outside much of the time, only being stored away in the hangars at weekends, when flying operations are rare

Inset The CAIM-9 pod simulates a Sidewinder missile for combat exercises. The versatile Hornet is capable of hauling 18,000 lbs of payload which might include the Sidewinder and Sparrow air-to-air missiles, Maverick and HARM air-to-ground weapons, Rockeye, Walleye and iron bombs, Harpoon anti-ship missiles and so on. The exact configuration depends on whether it's filling the fighter or attack role, but one standard piece of kit is the M61A1 Vulcan cannon

TransPac

Its position in the middle of the Pacific makes K-Bay an ideal stopping off point for Marine Corps aircraft travelling between the Far East and the continental USA. Trans-Pacific (TransPac) flights typically stay a day or two while the crews rest and the aircraft are refuelled and checked over

Providing a blast from the past, 'Specters' of VMFP-3, based at El Toro, give an idea of what the K-Bay ramp looked like when it was populated by F-4s. The 'Specters' should soon begin flying their own version of the Hornet, McDonnell Douglas currently working on the F/A-18(RC), a recce optimized version of the twin tub 'Delta' model

Above The Phantom IIs are returning home to the US following deployment in the Far East

Above Keeping cool: even shortly after a downpour the temperatures at K-Bay can soar. Most crews keep the canopies popped open until the last minute to avoid broiling in the heat

Left Waiting for the pattern to clear, two RF-4Cs hunker down on the taxiway while the runway is being used by returning F/A-18s. The Phantom IIs are starting the second leg of their journey home to El Toro

Prowler crews stretch their legs shortly after landing. These Grumman EA-6Bs of VMAQ-2 'Playboys' are normally based at Cherry Point, North Carolina, which is where they were headed after they'd rested

Essentially a derivative of the A-6 Intruder, the Prowler shares only 20 per cent parts commonality with its earlier relative. The EA-6 mission is electronic intelligence and counter-measures. In addition to the pilot, the aircraft carries three Electronics Counter-measures Officers (ECMO) whose job is to detect enemy radar—which might be directing missiles, anti-aircraft fire or fighters—and jam it

This page The aircraft are refuelled immediately, even through they may not be flying again for a day or two. This helps prevent water condensation in the gas tanks—a particularly common hazard in Hawaii's humid atmosphere

Right The forward avionics bay is just one of the many nooks and crannies that the crew uses to stow its luggage

A small concession to vanity, the flight leader's aircraft sports a black tail. This scheme harks back to former 'glory days' of VMAQ-2 when all squadron Prowlers wore jet-black tails and bold white Playboy bunnies

Far right Oxygen cylinders are taken from the Prowlers for replenishment

Ground crews give the Prowlers' systems a final once-over before closing down for the night

Right Hunched down on the transit hard stands, this KC-130F has finished its job of slaking the thirsts of the Prowlers. Also from Cherry Point, it provides backup and in-flight refuelling for the jets

Inset A C-9, one of two operating out of Cherry Point, has also escorted the Prowlers, carrying ground and ancillary personnel

With several Navy bases nearby, naval visitors are quite common. This C-9B Skytrain II from VR-59 has dropped in to pick up a consignment of VIPs. This particular C-9, christened CITY OF GRAND PRAIRIE, is regularly seen throughout the Pacific

The 'Frog'

The Boeing Vertol CH-46 Sea Knight is the standard troop and cargo hauler of the Marine Corps. Affectionately known as the 'Frog', it was developed to Marine Corps specs mainly to fit the beach assault role, operating off ships. Kaneohe Bay's machines are the Echo model which improved on the Delta spec by adding glassfibre rotor blades, crash-attenuating seats and a crash-resistant fuel system

Above Following a preflight briefing, 1st Lieutenant Don Bolender of HMM-262 walks out to co-pilot his aircraft on a training mission. Typical missions including troop transport, rappelling, SPIE, fire bucket and medevac hops

Right A crew chief gathers his intercom cable before climbing aboard the aircraft

Far right The avionics/radar bay open, the crew chief has a last-minute consultation with the ground crew before the mission

A Sea Knight taxies back to the ramp after landing at a helo pad. Unlike the Sea Stallions, the 'Frog' squadrons operate mainly from the special helo pads, although they may use the runway when the pads are busy, or when they need to go through the Bird Bath

Left A different kind of fire suppression: the 'Frogs' are often called upon to put out fires, not least when tracer rounds ignite the grass and foliage over at the rifle range. The large fire bucket is dunked in the sea and then, over the target, the water is released through a valve arrangement. The bucket is attached to the aircraft's winch through the centre hatch, known to the crews as the 'hell hole'

Right SPIE-rigging: Special Patrol Insertion/Extraction is a technique for getting combat teams into and out of small, 'hot' areas where a landing is impossible. A special cable fitted with hoops is lowered from the helo's 'hell hole' and the troops, wearing harnesses, attach themselves to it. They just have to hope that the pilot remembers he has them dangling below him! SPIE-rigging from the water is very rare, and no-one at K-Bay had seen it done before

A 'Frog' in the Bird Bath: the salty sea air creates all kinds of corrosion problems for K-Bay's helos. So incoming 'salty birds' are often directed by ground control through the Bird Bath—a set of automatic fresh water sprays. Here Lt Col Geier, CO of HMM-262, has taxied into position and is waiting a couple of minutes for his ship to be hosed down before proceeding back to the ramp

The clean aircraft taxies back to the ramp. Although the crew chief now has the side door down, it is speed limited and has to be closed for normal flight

The Sea Knight has been serving the Marine Corps since 1965, and it's only constant care that stops it showing its age. Although the Corps wants to replace it with the V-22 Osprey tilt-rotor, at the time these pictures were taken the future of the Osprey was in doubt, and the maintenance crews know they still have to get a lot of life out of their old Sea Knights. The box on the wing stub is a flare and chaff dispenser

Basking in the Hawaiian heat, the crews keep the engine covers, side doors and rear ramps open to prevent the aircraft turning into ovens

Search And Rescue

Search and Rescue is the responsibility of the Station Operations and
Maintenance Squadron (SOMS), which also handles general airfield operations.
SOMS has four of the specially-equipped SAR version of the HH-46D Sea Knight

The crew chief watches carefully for problems as the Sea Knight's two T58-GE-10 engines spool up. He's in direct contact with the pilot via the intercom cable running along the ground. Only when the aircraft is ready to depart will he jump on board and take his place by the door

Capt Roy Kompier, our helo driver, waits patiently for the rest of the crew to turn up, prior to flying a practice mission where he will rescue swimmers from the bay. One of the perks of the job is that SAR pilots get to fly more hours than the average 'Frog' driver—two hops a day is typical

Inset The SAR version of the Sea Knight is fitted with additional avionics and systems including a radar nav set and a hover and approach coupler, which makes it easier to maintain station over the target area

Right A K-Bay helo flown by Capt Kompier puts on an impressive demonstration of hoisting a litter from a moving boat during Armed Forces Day celebrations at Sand Harbor, Honolulu. The Sea Knight is ideal for this sort of manoeuvre as the twin-rotors make it less prone to weathercocking, so the rescue can be performed in any direction

Above The Navy patrol/rescue boat is doing about five knots—just enough to maintain headway. The helo must fly sideways, matching the boat's speed. Rotor wash can cause problems, but is less severe from the Sea Knight's twin fans than from single-rotor aircraft

Left During a practice session, the crew chief guides the litter aboard. Crewmen on board the boat help prevent the litter from swinging by using a control rope. The HH-46D is capable of carrying up to 12 litters, or 25 passengers

Crew chief Sgt Ken Layton calls directions to the pilot as the helo closes on the swimmers. The standard crew on SAR missions is four—pilot, co-pilot, crew chief and rescue swimmer. The swimmers were previously dropped into the water with the helo at 'ten and ten'—ten feet of altitude and a speed of ten knots

Right The crew's swimmer is the last to come up, having helped the other people get into the harness. Sometimes he will tag along with the last person to be hoisted

Inset The crew chief steadies the cable. Even with very smooth flying by the pilot, there can be a tendency for the cable to start swinging, which could be dangerous for everyone

Rescued: volunteers from a Navy installation at K-Bay provide bodies for the SAR teams to practice on. It is rumoured that Kaneohe Bay is a breeding ground for hammerhead sharks, but this is rarely pointed out to the volunteers

There is always at least one aircraft and crew on standby. Rescue missions are co-ordinated with the local Coast Guard and Navy installations, with K-Bay having responsibility for the East coast of Oahu. Many people—both military and civilian—owe their lives to the SAR crews

Special equipment on the HH-46 includes an external boom—mounted hoist capable of lifting 600 lbs at 300 feet per minute, a rescue strop and bubble windows for improved visibility. It also carries a rescue basket, floating rescue litter, jungle penetrator, loud hailer, two 12-man life rafts, and an SX16 nightsun searchlight

Sea Stallion

Left Kaneohe Bay's CH-53D Sea Stallions are operated by HMH-463. The Stallion's main mission is cargo resupply, although they will sometimes help out the Sea Knights with troop movements. HMH-463 birds generally stay pretty close to home, but there is the occasional ship deployment and six month rotation to MCAS Futenma, Okinawa, where they operate as Det-B

Below The Sea Stallion is the Marine Corps' main heavy lift vehicle. Developed by Sikorsky as the S-65, it entered Marine Corps service in 1966. Since then its undergone several upgrades, and the Delta model is now capable of hauling 37 troops or 8000 lbs of payload

Inset far right Capt Aron Gray, test pilot for HMH-463, checks the gauges as the twin General Electric T64-GE-413 engines of the CH-53D wind up to full power. Engine tests are commonplace as the Sea Stallions undergo constant maintenance

Inset The CH-53D's front office gives excellent visibility in all directions — including down. Instrumentation is fairly basic

Main picture A Sea Stallion steals home late. Take-offs and landings are generally performed on the active runway, which runs right alongside HMH-463's ramp

Main picture On these two 'slick' Sea Stallions the absence of tip tanks reveals that they used to be Alpha models, since reworked—with new engines and gearboxes—to Delta specification. On longer missions they are fitted with internal 318 gallon fuel tanks to increase range and loiter capability

Inset In the flight equipment office, spare bone domes and survival vests wait ready for visiting crewmembers. K-Bay regulars generally have their own kit kept in personal lockers

Left Kaneohe Bay is on the windward side of the island, and the trade winds can blow rough sometimes, so tying down rotor blades is more than customary—it's essential

Above Its engine covers gaping, a Sea Stallion receives some tender loving care from its ground crew. This particular CH-53 was built as a Delta model, as shown by the tip tanks which haul 650 gallons (4500 pounds) of fuel apiece

The two-tone camouflage is the current fashion and does at least provide some relief from the monotonous drab green. As they go through rework, all Sea Stallions are being repainted in the newer two-tone scheme

Maintenance crews make sure the squadron's ageing Delta models are fit to fly. The latest Echo model—with its extra rotor blade and engine and improved capacity—has yet to grace the K-Bay ramp, but with its current machines in such good shape there is no rush to replace them

Kaneohe Kaleidoscope

Above The ramp: the nearest hangar, No 101 which houses two Sea Knight squadrons, still bears the scars of the attack in 1941 which preceded the raid on Pearl Harbor by a few minutes. Further back are the F/A-18 hangars and the last one belongs to the Sea Stallions and is topped by the control tower. Beyond the present runway is the old wartime runway, now home to the Bird Bath and Combat Aircraft Loading Area

Right The Makapu Peninsula is effectively isolated from the rest of Oahu. The Nuupia Ponds to the right are crossed by only two roads, both protected by gates and sentries. In the distance the Ulupau Crater provides a naturally soundproofed arena for the rifle range. During the war it held three 14-inch guns salvaged from the USS *Arizona* which was sunk during the raid on Pearl Harbor. However, they were fired only once before the emplacement cracked and it was decided the mountain couldn't take the strain

Due to prevailing trade winds, 04 is usually the active runway. There is a distinct lack of overrun on what is already the smallest runway for tactical aircraft in the Navy and Marine Corps—just 7767 by 200 feet. It also has water at both ends and is crossed by an active road. All the same, it has been used by aircraft as large as the C-5 Galaxy. Four sets of arrestor gear are available for anybody with a hook and bad nerves, but they haven't been used much recently, and not at all since the Phantom IIs shipped out

Right The main control tower sits atop hangar 105. In 1946, this replaced the original wartime tower, which was located at the top of a small hill at the centre of the peninsula called Puu Hawaii Loa—but better known as Kansas Tower

Far right Air Traffic Control (ATC) for K-Bay is handled from a mobile trailer parked alongside the control tower. Signals are fed to if from radar equipment located on Kansas Tower. This is capable of extending its gaze for 200 miles, but the ATC crews are concerned mainly with traffic in a 35-mile radius

Marine Air Control Squadron 2 provides ATC facilities for MAG-24 when it's in the field. Mobile radar rooms like this can be loaded onto ships or trucks, into transport aircraft like the C-130 Hercules, or slung below Sea Stallions, and deployment takes only minutes

Below Part of the crews' conversion to the F/A-18 happens here, on the Operational Flight Trainer (OFT). Three large video monitors provide the visuals—night and dusk only—while banks of computers, including many identical to those in the real aircraft, simulate flight conditions. The simulator is used mainly for navigational and instrument training, emergency procedures and general familiarization

Right The OFT simulator faithfully replicates the Hornet's cockpit. The glass cockpit approach keeps buttons and switches to a minimum. The aircraft uses the HOTAS philosophy—'hands on throttle and stick'—meaning that most aircraft functions can be controlled using switches on the two controls. Although it doesn't move, inflating seat cushions help give an impression of G-forces, and the system hooks up to the pilot's G-suit and safety straps for even more realism

The Oshkosh P-19A fire trucks of the Crash Fire & Rescue crews stand ready to deal with any emergencies. Fortunately, their services are rarely needed, and the crews have to be content with frequent exercises to keep themselves sharp

Overleaf The main pump on the Oshkosh is capable of putting out 500 gallons of flame retardant foam every minute

The final cut

The Skyhawk used to be a familiar sight at K-Bay. For 16 years they shared the ramp with the F-4s — now they're all gone. The aircraft pictured here were performing their last few sorties before shipping out forever

Above and right The Skyhawks belonged to Marine Air Logistics Squadron 24 'Bandits', which is now without aircraft. The 'Scooters' were used for a variety of roles, including training and as 'enemy' aircraft in mock combat. Now when K-Bay's Hornets go looking for trouble they mix it up with VC-1 'Blue Alii' A-4s and TA-4s from nearby Naval Air Station Barbers Point

At the time these pictures were taken, only five Skyhawks remained at K-Bay. All were destined for the Navy—two weeks later four had joined VF-127 'Cylons' at NAS Fallon and one went to VF-126 'Bandits' at Miramar. They will be used mainly as target tugs

Left The Skyhawks were in great demand by the fighter squadron crews while they waited for delivery of their Hornets, and by others who wanted to build up stick time on fast jets

Above Utilization of the Skyhawks was pretty heavy, with an average of two, two-ship sorties a day — right up to the day they left

Above Blasting out: with the Pratt & Whitney J52-P-8A delivering 9300 pounds of thrust, and the aircraft lightly laden, the 'Scooter' fairly hops off the runway

Right With the 'Scooters' following the F-4s into K-Bay's past, the base will quieten down somewhat. The GE-404 engines on the Hornets are significantly less noisy than its predecessors' power plants

These Phantom IIs have seen better days. Both ex-VMFA-232 F-4Ss, they sit in a patch of waste ground off the side of the runway, used only by Crash Fire & Rescue teams to practice aircraft evacuations and firefighting

K-Bay hung on to its Phantom IIs right to the end. VMFA-212 'Lancers' was one of
the last front line squadrons to turn in its F-4Ss for Hornets

Providing a glimpse of past splendours, one of VMFA-212's old F-4s guards the flight line. Bearing the name of the MAG CO—Col Gary 'Filthy' Elsten—it's the only fast jet on the base which isn't painted in air superiority grey

The ubiquitous Beech

The UC-12B is a common sight on Marine Corps airfields these days. The military derivative of the Beech Super King Air 200, it's used mainly for ferrying VIPs and other general purpose work

This UC-12B is operated by the Station Operations and Maintenance Squadron and is used by SOMS's helicopter pilots—who normally fly the SAR helos—to keep up their fixed-wing hours

'Down in the weeds (and the water)'

The Kahuku training ground, up at the northern tip of Oahu, is a large area of forest and hills used by the Army and Marine Corps for infantry training. These grunts from 1st Platoon, Kilo-3-3 (K company, 3rd Battalion, 3rd Marine Regiment), are getting ready to defend a hill against an 'attack' by the 2nd and 3rd platoons

Inset A grunt from the 3rd Battalion sports the M-16 fitted with an M-203 grenade launcher. Infantry units might spend anything from two to ten days in the field, having been dropped there by CH-46s from Kaneohe Bay

Main picture Digging in on Hill 534, a member of 1st Platoon puts up camouflage as the unit waits to be attacked. It turned out to be unnecessary—the attacking units chose the wrong hill and were sitting ducks for the 1st Platoon. Later that night all units were flown home by K-Bay's helos

Left During M-60 machine gun qualifications, grunts from Alpha and Bravo Companies, 1st Battalion, 3rd Marine Regiment don first-level MOPP gear. The 'Mission Oriented Protective Posture' equipment is protection against chemical warfare

Right The US Marine Corps doesn't have special forces as such, but the Recon outfits come pretty close. Qualified as parachutists, divers and swimmers, they can tackle just about anything. As part of their relentless training, Recon divers prepare to wade into the surf on one of the Mokapu Peninsula's beautiful beaches

Even in diving gear the Marines can't resist wearing green! A Recon diver gets ready to take the plunge